Christopher Flagellan

A funeral discourse occasioned by the much lamented death of

Mr. Yorick

Christopher Flagellan

A funeral discourse occasioned by the much lamented death of Mr. Yorick

ISBN/EAN: 9783743491564

Manufactured in Europe, USA, Canada, Australia, Japa

Cover: Foto ©ninafisch / pixelio.de

Manufactured and distributed by brebook publishing software
(www.brebook.com)

Christopher Flagellan

A funeral discourse occasioned by the much lamented death of

Mr. Yorick

A
FUNERAL DISCOURSE,

Occasioned by the much lamented

DEATH of Mr. YORICK,

Prebendary of Y - - k

and

Author *of the much admired* LIFE *and* OPINIONS
of TRISTRAM SHANDY,

PREACHED

before a very mixed

Society of JEMMIES, JESSAMIES,

Methodists and Christians,

AT

A NOCTURNAL MEETING

in PETTICOAT LANE,

and now published

at the unanimous Request of the Hearers

BY

CHRISTOPHER FLAGELLAN, A. M.

and enriched with the

NOTES OF VARIOUS COMMENTATORS.

Ambubaiarum Collegia, Pharmacopolæ
Mendici, Mimæ, Balatrones, hoc genus omne
Mæstum ac sollicitum est Doctoris morte Tigelli.

HORAT. Sat. II. L. I. 2. 3.

LONDON:
Printed for W. NICOLL in St. Pauls Church Yard.
MDCCLXI.

Advertifement.

Whereas it has been maliciously, *or rather* stupidly *reported, that the late* Mr. ST--E, *alias* YORICK, *is not dead, but that, on the contrary, he is writing a* Fifth *and* Sixth, *and has carried his Plan as far as a* Fiftieth *and* Sixtieth *Volume of the Book, called* The Life and Opinions of Triftram Shandy; *This is to give Notice, to all whom it may or may not concern, that this Report is absurd, improbable, false and groundless, as will evidently appear to such as read, with any degree of attention, the following Difcourfe.* --- *If, therefore, such* Fifth *and* Sixth, *or* Fiftieth *and* Sixtieth *pretended Volumes of the aforefaid Book fhould appear in the Shop of any Bookfeller or Bookfellers, the Publick may be affured, that they are not the production of the late* Mr. ST--E, *but are rather to be attributed to his Ghaftly Ghoft, which is faid to walk in the Purlieus of Covent-Garden and Drury-Lane. And the faid Publick is moreover intreated to fet on foot a profecution of fuch Bookfeller or Bookfellers for thus carrying on an intercourfe and correfpondence with* Evil Spirits.

499904

Dedication.

To the Right Honourable;

The Lord F---G

and

to the very Facetious

Mr. FOOTE;

My Lord *and* — Sir,

The *Fool's cap*, put upon Socra-
tes, did not appear more in-
congruous and ill-placed, than the
Dedication, of the *Life and Opinions
of Triſtram Shandy*, which was im-
poſed upon his Anti-type William
Pitt, Eſqr. To avoid therefore an
impropriety of this nature, and to put

it

it out of any malevolent Critick's power to fay to me,

———— *pergis pugnantia fecum Frontibus adverfis componere,*

HORACE.

I have taken the Liberty, My Lord and — Sir, to lay at your feet the following Tragi-comical Effufions of a heart which is affected, as it ought to be, by the death and annihilation of the late Mr. *St--e*, alias *Yorick*. If you fhould inquire into the particular reafon of this Dedication, I hope your curiofity will be fatisfied, when I tell you, that it is entirely owing to the protection which this *Eminent Divine* received from the PEER, and the refemblance he bore to the COMEDIAN.

I am, MY LORD and — Sir,

Your moft humble and obedient Servant,
CHRISTOPHER FLAGELLAN.

A second, but short Advertisement.

The Notes, that are Printed with the following Discourse, were composed by the learned Friends of Mr. FLAGELLAN, *who perused it in Manuscript. The Editor has published at the End of Each Note, the name of the Critick to whom the Publick is indebted for it. The References and Citations are owing to the labour of Mr.* FLAGELLAN *himself.*

The Text is to be found in the firſt Volume of the Goſpel of the Jemmies, otherwiſe called the Life and opinions of Triſtram Shandy, at theſe words:

ALASS POOR YORICK!

My Brethren,

A certain curate in the famous city of Paris, being appointed to preach the Funeral Sermon of this Metropolitan, began his diſcourſe in the following manner: " *dearly beloved brethren* " *and fellow chriſtians* (ſaid he fetching a heavy " ſigh from the very bottom of his heart) " *there are but two things that embaraſs me at* " *this time in the place where I ſtand, and that* " *render difficult the taſk I have undertaken.* " *The firſt of theſe is the* LIFE *of his grace,* " *and the ſecond his* DEATH. *His manner of* " *living and his manner of dying are the only ob-* " *jections that can be brought againſt his cha-* " *racter, and were it not for theſe two croſs,* " *though trifling circumſtances, nothing would* " *have been wanting to render my panegyrick*

B " *com-*

" *compleat.*" To prevent my falling into the
perplexity of this fimple curate I fhall throw
a veil over the life of the mortal author of
Triſtram Shandy, fince the beſt way of con-
quering difficulties, as well as temptations is
by avoiding them. Were we to enter into a
detail of the actions, incidents, events, circumſtances, exploits, difappointments, intrigues,
attempts, plans, affairs, and tricks that make
up the motley tablature of his life, *(a)* both
their nature and their number would entirely
overpower us, and it would be difficult for us
to know, where we ſhould begin or where we
ſhould end the whimſical ſtory. But it is his
death, that we propoſe as the gloomy ſubject
of our preſent meditations. If, however, my
dear brethren, you defire to have fome faint
notion of this man, you will find a fmall
fketch of his *origin,* and *character* in a certain

(a) It has been too often the failing of orators to
facrifice, what may be called, ſtrict and rigorous truth
to the harmony and cadence of their periods. Mr. FLA-
GELLAN feems to have run a little into this defect, to
render his *ennumeration,* (a very powerful trope in ora-
tory!) more ſtriking. The life of YORICK was not fo
variegated as he feems to imagine. *Tibbaldius Maximus.*

repofitory of literary intelligence, which is well known and juftly efteemed. Thefe *literati* tell us that this author was a fon of *Comus*; *(b)* which muft be underftood undoubtedly, in a figurative and allegorical fenfe, becaufe it is well known, that *Yorick*, alias St—n, was born of chriftian parents, however ftrongly appearances may feem to infinuate the contrary. When therefore, his admirers call him a fon of *Comus*, they probably mean no more than this, that he was a lover of his belly, his bottle, and his joke, and was no enemy to noƈturnal dancing, *(c)* which latter circumftance appears probable enough from his ftory of the *old-clock*. When Doƈtor Yorick publifhed his fermons, the learned panegyrifts, now mentioned, fhouted for joy and exprefled themfelves upon the occafion in the following manner. *It is with pleafure we behold this* Son *of* Comus (i. e. the Reverend

N O T E S.

(b) See the *Critical Review* Vol. IX. No. 52.

(c) See Fabri *Thefaurus*, at the word Comus, Pomey's *Pantheon*, King's *mythology*, Bower's *Hiftory of the Popes*, and Echard's *caufes of the contempt of the clergy.*

Doƈtor,

(4)

Doctor, whose death we lament) *descending from the chair of mirth and frolick, to inspire sentiments of piety, and read lectures of morality to that very audience, whose hearts he had captivated with good natured wit and facetious humour.* (d) This very remarkable passage, my brethren, occasioned some mistakes. It led many people to imagine that our YORICK was by *profession* a buffoon or a comick actor, and that he had once on a time condescended to put on a grave face, and to pen a *sermon* in place of a *farce*, they imagined that the *chair of mirth and frolick* was his usual residence, (e) and that he had mounted the *pulpit*, to astonish as well as to edify the audience, which he had diverted on the theatre. This notion however specious, nay true in several respects, is yet upon the whole false and groundless, for it is well known, that YORICK was a preacher metamorphosed into a buffoon, and not a

NOTES.

(d) See the CRITICAL REVIEW, Vol. IX. No. 5². for May 1760.

(e) And so it was, says the learned and comical FUNKIGIUS in his facetious History of the nature, origin and decline of Bartlemy Fair.

buffoon

buffoon converted into a preacher. *(f)* **The**
fame panegyrifts give feveral other hints concerning this jovial and frolickfome *fucceffor of*
the Apoftles, which may contribute to give
fome idea of his life, though that, indeed, is
fufficiently known. But we repeat it again,
it is his death that muft occupy our thoughts
at prefent, and this will afford matter enough
for this difcourfe.

(f) There is here an evident miftake in Mr. FLAGEL-
LAN's ftory of the cafe. For nature had made *Yorick* a
buffoon before the pious and ardent hope of a *fat* living
had transformed him into a clergyman. This feigned
character, as is well known, fat very ill upon him, fo that
even in his very fermons every one could difcern the
marks of a ftrong propenfity to fall back into his natural
bent. At laft he fell plump into the bofom of nature
and declared his jovial relapfe to the world by publifhing
the Life and Opinions of *Triftram Shandy.* Whether he
was then a clergyman converted into a buffoon, or rather remained both one and the other, is a queftion that
muft de decided in the affirmative or negative according
to the definition we give of the term *clergyman.* As Mr.
FLAGELLAN has refolved this queftion in another part
of this difcourfe, we fhall refer the reader to his obfer-
vations.

To

To proceed then with order in treating this unparelleled fubject we fhall, in the 1ft. place prove, dont be furprized gentle reader, that the Rev. *Dr. Yorick* alias St—n, is dead, yea dead. 2dly. we fhall confider this lamentable event with refpect to thofe focieties or individuals to whom it is a moft affecting and irreparable lofs, 3dly. we fhall anfwer the various objections that have been mouthed and handed about againft the deceafed, and fhall conclude with an *improper* application of the whole.

1 Firft then I am to prove that the Reverend Dr. YORRICK, is — ah! what do I fay! — dead ; dead indeed ? — yea, dead. — Some fingular circumftances of this fatal exit will alfo come naturally under this firft head.

The deplorable and ever to be lamented death of Dr. YORRICK. ——— *Why, Sir,* (will fome of my cavilling hearers fay within themfelves) *the man is fill alive.* Patience, gentle hearer, whoever though art that indulgeft this unbelieving thought, patience for a moment,—— pray what do you call *life?* you will perhaps anfwer, that every body knows
what

what *life* is; but I am very far from being of that opinion. You will fay, that *life* is a certain ftate of —— that, in fhort, it is to be *alive*, and that you faw Dr. YORRICK in the tavern yefterday with his wig under the table, drinking in a fparkling brimmer *the beft in Chriftendom*. We grant the fact; we only alledge that it does not give any force to your objection; for had you feen him moving, eating, drinking, digefting, and evacuating, this would not, taken altogether, amount to a proof that he was *alive*. Did you never hear of the famous duck of the ingenious *Vaucanfon*, which performed all thefe *animal* functions with the greateft facility and precifion, and yet —— was no more than a piece of wood curioufly wrought, according to mechanical principles, by that admirable artift. —— But that you may not look upon this as a mere evafion let us enter more deeply into the matter; for we live in a ftrange fceptical age, in which the plaineft truths are called in queftion, and felf-evident propofitions are looked upon as problematical. One denies the exiftence of *motion*, another that of *matter*, and a third that

of

of *spirit*. A famous Scotch philosopher, who
has for many years past, been blowing with
great self-complacence, pretty, glittering, daz-
zling bubbles of metaphysick into the atmos-
phere of science, has denied the connexion
between *cause* and *effect*, (g) and even called
in question the existence of *body* and *spirit*. (h)
It will not then be wondered that, in this discourse, I set myself to prove such an evident
and palpable truth as the death of poor *Yorick*,
and if I am obliged to be more learned and
logical upon this point, than is usual in ser-
mons, the fault must be charged upon the in-
credulity and scepticism of the times.

To remove at the same time all subject of
chicane ; I shall explain, 1st. what I do not
mean and 2dly, what I do mean when I say
that Dr. YORRICK *is dead.* ―

N O T E S.

(g) See the essay upon power in a certain bundle of
intricacies entitled *Philosophical essays upon human under-
standing*.

(h) See a *treatise upon human nature* by the same author in 2 large volumes 8vo. which have been little read
and less understood.

First

Firſt then *negatively*, when I ſay that Yorick
is dead, I do not mean, that he is yet ſo far
dead as to be in the caſe required by the will
of a late teſtator whoſe effects were to be tranſ-
mitted to a ſecond heir when the firſt was
breathleſs, rotten, and *damned*. (*i*) I do not
even pretend to ſay that our deceaſed Doctor
ought to be buryed in any other grave than
that of oblivion, where he now lies low; for
were his body laid ſix foot under ground, the
ſons of Themis might pronounce, that he was
buried alive.— What I mean then 2dly, and
poſitively, is, that of the two principal kinds
of life diſtinguiſhed by the epithets of *animal*
and *ſpiritual*, or (to ſpeak more philoſophi-
cally) *brutal* and *intellectual*, the former alone
is poſſeſſed by YORICK, in whom the *animal*
lives, while the *man* is dead. Perhaps, dearly
beloved, you may here again deceive your-
ſelves and imagine I mean, that YORICK is
dead in treſpaſſes and ſins. No, no, that is
not my meaning; for were this true in fact,
it is the caſe of many, as well as of him, and

(*i*) See the *Daily Advertiſer*.

C   this

this circumftance alone would not furnifh a
fufficient pretext for preaching, with fo much
folemnity, his funeral fermon. That is but a
mere *moral death*, which, in the opinion of
our times, does not hinder a man from ap-
pearing found, lively, and well, or from being efteemed a good citizen, a good compa-
nion, a good friend, a good author, a good
minifter, a good bifhop, a good methodift,
a good every thing, in fhort, but a good
chriftian, which laft character has long ceafed
to be an object of private ambition or publick efteem. Befides, it has been conjectured
by fome deep thinkers, that the *moral part* of
YORICK's foul was *ftill-born*, (k) and that he
never enjoyed any kind of life, but the *animal*
and *intellectual*. Now if this be the cafe, he
cannot be dead in trefpaffes or fins or morally
dead, for to fuppofe a man *morally dead*, im-

(k) See a difcourfe formerly publifhed by the learned
and pious Dr. SECKER, (now Lord Arch-Bifhop of
Canterbury) *de Partu Difficili*. See alfo, EPAPHRODITVS
BULFINGER de *Generatione Animorum Lib* vi. *Cap.* 89.

plies

plies evidently that he was once *morally alive*. (*l*) It is at leaſt, certain that his father, who was a good man, intended that his ſon ſhould be a chriſtian and even deſigned him for a ghoſtly profeſſion ; with this view he brought him to church to have him received into the congregation of the faithful. But—O! marvellous and ominous event! the wayward infant, after the example of the Emperor CONSTANTINE COPRONYMUS eaſed himſelf in the baptiſmal fount, which was looked upon as a preſage of his future contempt of religion and morality, and was interpreted as if he had ſaid a f—— for both.

To return then to our ſubject (for peace to the departed *ſpirit* of YORICK he has

N O T E.

(*l*) Dr. FLAGELLAN ſeems to reaſon here much in the manner of the late excellent Dr. SHERLOCK Biſhop of London. Every one will not underſtand this note.

much infected us with the itch of digreffions) we lament the death of YORICK's better
part, 'that part which was the vehicle of
judgment and wit. That this *part* was not
ftill-born is manifeft from the excellent fermons that appeared to the world under his
name, and that it is now totally dead appears as evidently from the Book entitled,
the Life and opinions of *Triftram Shandy*, and
more efpecially from the III and IV Volumes, we may fay the *laft* of that wonder-
ful performance. In the two firft Volumes
of this work, YORICK appeared fick and
declining, yet certain fparks of intellectual
fire flew out here and there, which prevent-
ed our looking upon his wit, as utterly eva-
porated; nay, there feemed to be fome
hopes of its recovery, notwithftanding the
long fits of abfence, perplexity and delirium
into which it had fallen. But no fooner did
the two laft Volumes appear, than all the
fons of drollery yawned over the witlefs,
fenfelefs, lifelefs page, and ftriking their

penfive

penſive boſoms, ſaid within themſelves, Yo-
RICK is no more what he was, and of his
recovery there is no hope. They ſaw his
wit labouring, tugging, ſtriving for life,
but all to no purpoſe. They ſaw it ſinking
under every effort to keep it alive, and ob-
ſerved that the *Hiſtory of Noſes* or SLAW-
KENBERGIUS's *tale* inſtead of raiſing it
above the water, made it ſink much deeper,
and preſented to the reader the moſt amaz-
ing, unintelligible jumble of words, that
perhaps has been penned or pronounced
either in ancient or modern times. They
lamented the total extinction of poor Yo-
RICKS judgment and the abſolute annihilation of his wit, ſucceeded by dreadful fits
of raving in which he evacuated many in-
coherent and obſcure words and ſentences.
Theſe ſentences multiplied prodigiouſly the
number of head achs among the good people of England, who ſtrained the fibres
of their anxious brains to find wit among
the excrements of a dying genius.

YORICK

YORICK, himself, perceived the approaching end of his intellects ; yet from the eager thirst of fame that confumed him, he endeavoured to conceal the matter. He called about him in his laft moments his friends and intimates, and addreffed to them the following Difcourfe :

" *Jemmies, Bucks, Peers,* and *Parfons.*
" Hear the laft words of Poor YORICK.
" — You fee me here, Gentlemen, in a
" moft pitiful plight, — in the condition
" of one who made his court to *fame,* af-
" pired after *wit,* and is now upon the
" point of being abandoned by both. I
" have been well informed, that the pu-
" blick, which, you know, is a many-
" headed, and confequently a fickle, Mon-
" fter, has begun to turn its applaufe into
" contempt, and my works having no lon-
" ger the merit of novelty, nor the poig-
" nancy of wit, are like to meet with a ve-
" ry

" ry bad fate. This, I own, goes to my
" heart.——The *hatred* of man I value not
" ——but I cannot ſtand firm againſt *con-*
" *tempt.* When an old-faſhioned ſociety of
" *Monthly Criticks,* (*n*) who have undertak-
" en to maintain the deſperate cauſe of
" good ſenſe, good writing, and common
" decency, attacked me with ſerious re-
" monſtrances, and aſſerted that a *Doctor of*
" *Divinity* made an abſurd figure in the
" form of a harlequin and an obſcene buf-
" foon, you know how lightly I treated that
" admonition, and how little I was affect-
" ed with the inconſiſtency that there real-
" ly was between my jocoſe writings and

N O T E.

(*n*) Dr. Y o r i c k means here the authors of
the Monthly Review, and alludes to their admirable extract of his ſermons. An extract, in
which ſatire appeared with dignity, and in which,
alſo, the moſt lively wit was employed in the ſer-
vice of decency and virtue. *Roſarius Philologicus*
& Philaretus.

my

" my ghoſtly character. All this, howe-
" ver it might ruffle my *jerkin*, did not
" once touch the *lining*. (*o*) Thanks to
" Comus and Bacchus, I am tolerably hard
" within; and as long as my *animal ſpi-*
" *rits* were in a glow, and their motions
" were ſupported by *good eatirg*, with
" mirth and jollity, I never minded what a
" parcel of old, muſty, Cromwellian Di-
" vines uſed to call the *four laſt things*. (*p*)

N O T E S.

(*o*) See p. 13 and 16 of the III. Volume of
the much-forgotten book entitled *The Life and Opi-*
nions of Triſtram Shandy.

(*p*) As the *Four laſt things* are not much known
in this age, it may not be improper to inform the
reader, that by them are meant *death, judgment,*
beaven and *hell.* Commentators are not all agreed
concerning the reaſon why they are called *the four*
loſt things. They muſt undoubtedly be ſo named,
either becauſe they are *indeed* the very *laſt things*
that People generally think of, or, becauſe, in the
order of time, they conclude the tranſitory drama
of this preſent life. *Warburtonius.*

How

" How long I may be proof againſt the
" clamours of ſome biſhops, who, I am
" told, are Chriſtians, and againſt the re-
" monſtances of an *inward monitor*, who
" has not the courage to follow me thro'
" thick and thin, I cannot tell. For if
" *contempt* comes, 1 ſhall be dejected ;——
" if I am dejected, I ſhall *think*, and if I
" think, my repoſe is at an end. So, Gen-
" tlemen, for G--d's ſake ſave me from
" *contempt*, or elſe I am undone. ———
" You know what obligations you are un-
" der to me, *(here he began te ſcb and ſigh)*
" I have turned myſelf into all ſhapes to
" procure you amuſement, and to enable
" you to kill the heavy moments. I have
" joined together the moſt jarring and he-
" terogeneous forms to make you laugh.
" I have converted my *buſhy wig* into a
" *fool's cap*, my venerable caſſock into a
" pickle-herring's particoloured veſt ; I
" have boxed the compaſs of facetiouſneſs
" and drollery to diſtend your lungs and
" chear your ſpirits. I ſtrained —— and

" ftrained —— all my brainftrings to force
" wit from art, when nature refufed it.
" I have incurred the indignation of all
" good Chriftians; and acted as if *religion*
" were a —— (pray filence within, impor-
" tunate monitor !) I was faying — gen-
" tlemen, that I have acted as if *religion*
" was a *farce* to gain your favour. I have
" facrificed the gravity of my profeffion,
" the demands of my miniftry, the efteem
" of the wife (*here he feemed to be feized with*
the gripes or with fome internal paroxyfm that
produced a fimilar effect, even a dreadful wry
face, which, added to the natural afperity of
his faturnine vifage, made him grin horribly,
and conceal his agony in a ghaftly fmile) to
" prop — prop — propagate the reign of
" mirth in your nocturnal focieties.——
" *Mifcebam facra profanis.* —— and after
" all, notwithftanding how fafhionable it
" is to be fenfelefly profane, I fear *contempt,*
" —— Contempt is going to purfue me
" —— and the inward monitor tells me
" I deferve it. Oh ! gentlemen and ladies
guard

" guard me againſt contempt. ————

" Contempt———— contempt———— (*here*
he began to rave) in Latin, *contemptus*————
" in French, *mépris*———— Stand off, thou
" heart-dejecting ſpectre ———— Where
" ſhall I take refuge ? ———— Where !
" ah where ! In the walls of *Namur*, for-
" tified by uncle Toby ! Ah !—Slop—
" avaunt———— who knows whether my
" friend F o o t e will not abandon me——
" take me off as he has done *Whitefield*,
" and thus exhibit to pit, box, and galle-
" ries the two extremes of folly ! ————

When our poor friend, my dear brethren, had continued ſometime in this wretched ſtate, he came to himſelf a little, and
one of his intimate companions aſked him
why he feared contempt ſo much, ſince his
book had been ſo graciouſly received by the
publick. Why, Y o r i c k, ſaid he, was
ever book attended with ſuch favourable
circumſtances as yours? It was dedicated

to

to a minifter *(q)*, read by the clergy *(r)*, approved of by the wits *(s)*, ftudyed by the

N O T E S.

(q) It was, indeed, dedicated to the right and truly honourable WILLIAM PITT Efq; The *proprie-ty* of this dedication ftruck the judicious part of man-kind very much, and recalled to their remembrance feveral very famous dedications, in which the fame kind of aptitude and decorum reigned ; among o-thers a treatife upon the fweets of *arbitrary* power to CATO of *Utica*, a diflertation upon the *Grecian Dance* to CATO the *Cenfor* ; the pleafures of a *fpiri-tual feaft* to the late arch-bifhop of Y - - k ; the hiftory of the *Goths and Vandals* to the *Earl of* BUTE ; .and to name but three more, *Machiavel's Prince* to his Majefty *King* GEORGE *the third*, an eflay upon *plain-dealing* to the *French miniftry*, and a fenti-mental difcourfe upon the pleafures of *chaftity* to the *emprefs of Ruffia.*

(r) The late arch-bifhop of Y**k, Dr. G*****t of leaden memory, ufed to fay, that he was fo delight-ed with the life and opinions of Triftram Shandy, that he read them once every fix weeks. Did he preach as often ? No. *Poppius Ficinus.*

(s) A learned, or rather judicious critick imagines that there is here an error of the prefs, and that in-ftead of *Wits*, we muft read *Witlings. Bentliculus.*

mer-

merchants, gazed at by the ladies, and was become the pocket-companion of the nation. Besides, it procured you a benefice (*t*), and enriched Mr. *Dodsley*.

At the name of *Dodsley*, YORICK lifted a feeble eye, resumed strength, recollected all his fire to express his indignation, looked aghast for some moments — and uttered in broken accents the words which follow :

" Dodsley --name fatal to YORICK -- and
" ominous to the Shandean race — Dodsley
" has been my ruin. — It is to him I owe
" my death — the approaching annihilation
" of my thinking substance. It is owing
" to him, that I am soon to be no more
" than a material mass, moved by *animal*
" *spirits*, whose fermentation will be called

N O T E.

(*t*) Yorick's friend is surely mistaken here, it is scarcely possible in the nature of things, that Yorick should have received a benefice as a recompense for the book here under consideration. Otherwise we may hope to see Mr. *Foote* one day Arch-Bishop of Canterbury. The question is in whose gift the benefice was, aye, that indeed, is the question. See *the dedication.*

life,

" life, and accompanied with *memory*, which
" metaphyficians look upon as *corporal*.
" *Dodfley* has been my ruin — he has forced
" *wit*, which will not be forced, and has
" cracked the ftrings of my intellect by
" drawing them too violently. I gave
" him two Volumes of pretty good ftuff,
" and the unexpected fale of them made
" him yawn after twenty. Twenty faid
" I, — Mr. *Dodfley*—that cannot be.—It is
" impoffible to hold out fo long in the
" ftrain, upon which I began. It is too ex-
" traordinary to be.——No matter what ftrain
" you write in, *replied the judicious book-*
" *feller*; it is now become the *mode* to ad-
" mire you ;—the giddy part of the nation
" are your zealous patrons, and the public
" voice is in your favour ;—therefore what-
" ever you difgorge, were your productions
" nothing more than the wretched crudi-
" ties of a difturbed brain, they will be fwal-
" lowed with avidity, provided——aye, *faid*
" *I*, I underftand you, provided they be
" larded with a little bawdy, nicely gawzed
" over, and feafoned with a proper mix-

" ture

" ture of impiety and profanenefs.————

" That is not all, Sir,— *replied the man-*

" *midwife of the republick of letters*, I add

" another provifo, that you continue to fol-

" low a rule, which you have tolerably well

" obferved in your two firft volumes. That

" rule is, that when *wit* does not flow, you

" muft become *unintelligible* rather than con-

" tinue *infipid.*—Obfcurity, Sir, is an admi-

" rable thing ; it excites refpect, and ma-

" ny of your readers will admire you in pro-

" portion as they ceafe to underftand you.

" By the fpecimens they have had of your

" wit they will conclude that where the

" wit does not ftrike them, as for example

" in your intended *chapter of nofes*, it muft

" be their fault, and not yours, they will

" fuppofe that this fame wit lies like truth

" in a well, and they will laugh with a fool-

" lifh of praife at every thing you fay, pro-

" vided it be thrown with a happy air of

" eafe and impudence. *Obfcurity*, Sir, I

" repeat it, is an admireble thing, and it

" has given reputation to many an au-

" thor.

" thor.———'Pray Master Y O R I C K are
" you so much deceived with respect to the
" truth of things, as to imagine that your
" two first Volumes were admired only for
" their w't? — Wit indeed there was in
" them more or less—some striking images
" of a ludicrous kind; and though you
" had no principal figures that made a true
" composition, yet the corners of your
" picture presented here and there enter-
" taining decorations. But after all, Sir,
" wit was not the only thing that drew ap-
" plause. ODDITY was the bait that hook-
" ed in the gaping multitude.—Oddity in
" the author who united the two most con-
" tradictory characters : *Oddity* in the book,
" which, certainly resembles nothing that
" ever was, or ever will be, which is with-
" out any design moral or immoral, and
" is no more, indeed, than a combination
" of notions, facts, and circumstances,
" that terminate in—*nothing*. So then, Sir,
" give me twenty Volumes more of this
" same brilliant, striking, interesting *noth-*
" *ing*. It is wonderfully suited to the taste
" of

" of the age; it will tickle the wanton,
" amuse the unthinking, countenance the
" profane, and carry on to perfection that
" spirit of trifling that makes such a rapid
" progress among us. At the same time,
" my Reverend Buck, I have no objection
" to your being as witty as you please;—
" none at all—and here, said he, (chinking
" a long green purse full of yellow boys)
" here is the source of wit, the dispenser
" of genius, the master of arts, and not
" the belly alone, as juvenal falsely ima-
" gined. (u)

" So spoke D--sl-y, and these his last
" words, were to my ears what Hertford-
" shire cyder is to a thirsty soul, a roasted
" sirloin to a craving stomach, or a
" plump - - - - partridge to a keen hun-
" ter. I swallowed inconsiderately the
" bate——I fell a writing, and a writing,

N O T E.

(u) Magister Artis et Ingeni Largitor, Venter.

E   " like

" like a certain Doctor who has invented
" more remedies than there are difeafes. I
" flowed muddy, like *Lucilius*, and as I
" wrote upon *nothing*, *i. e.* upon no given
" fubject of any kind, fo every thing was
" equally adapted to my purpofe. Thus
" then I went on without time or reaſon,
" writing through thick and thin, flying
" like the people of Strafburgh, here and
" there——in at one door, out at another——
" this way and that way——long ways
" and crofs ways——till unfortunately one
" of the multitude, who had followed me
" through two Volums laughing and ap-
" plauding, took it into his head one day
" to afk himfelf what he had been ap-
" plauding.—— An unhappy queftion for
" me——my dear friends, —— for upon
" examining himfelf he found, that, nine
" times in ten, he had been applauding
" through meer *fympathy*, which (accord-
" ing to the learned and ingenious Mr.
" SMITH) is the fupreme mover and gover-
" nor general of all our moral fentiments
" and

" and affections; (w) he found, to ex-
" plain the thing lefs metaphyfically, that
" it was become modifh and epidemical to
" laugh and admire in read ng my book,
" and that he was involuntarily feized with
" the general contagion.——In fhort—he
" would laugh no more——and——from
" that moment I date my ruin; for the
" contagion changed fides againft me : the
" man, now mentioned, put the fame que-
" ftion to others that he had put to him-
" felf, and it was anfwered in the fame
" manner. At the appearance, and reading
" of my third and fourth Volume, every man
" fhrugged his fhoulders——compofed his
" features towards an air of *contempt*, of
" which I have been myfe f the melancho-
" ly witnefs. A few of my friends endea-
" voured to maintain my caufe; they read,

N O T E.

(w) See *the Theory of Moral Sentiments* by Mr.
ADAM SMITH, Profeffor of Moral Philofophy in the
Univerfity of Glafgow.

" but

" but——yawned, and the forced laugh
" was interrupted in the middle by a wide
" gape, which formed a contraſt of fea-
" tures ridiculous beyond meaſure. ——
" Thus, Gentlemen, I am undone.——
" My eputation is gone——fame indeed
" ſpreads my name abroad, but it is alaſs!
" with her *poſterior* trumpet;——my infant
" Triſtram is ſmothered in his cradle ; Dr.
" SLOP pinched off his noſe, and the pub-
" lick, which were deſigned to be his nurſ-
" ing-mothers, have over laid him through
" neglect.——Sic tranſit gloria mundi-——
" let us eat and drink and drink for to
" morrow we die.——(*Here after ſome violent*
" *fits of raving.* YORICK *breathed out his*
" *intellectual part.*")

Thus expired the glory of YORICK ,
whoſe exiſtence is now reduced to matter
and motion, and here. —My brethren let us
pauſe,—— to pauſe is wiſe—— and were I ſo
happy as to have imbibed a portion of that
ſpirit whoſe extinction we lament, I ſhould
not fail to give you a learned digreſſion
upon

upon paufes.——*Paufes* indeed are ftriking things——as you will be convinced if you go to hear the great orators at Drury-Lane Monkwell-Street, &c.——There is a paufe of prudence which embellifhes a void, and makes the fpeaker appear eloquent when he has nothing to fay.——There is a paufe of application, which enforces what has been faid——and there is a paufe of preparation to draw attention to what is yet to be faid. (x)

My

N O T E.

(x) Mr. FLAGELLAN while he was repeating this triple diftinction of paufes, looked his part admirably, and reprefented, with exquifite expreffion, the three different paufes by a triple modification of his moft fignificant countenance.——I wifh the Printer could have given us an image of this!——but how print a paufe, or the looks that accompany it?——This defect in the art of printing offers a very ftriking, and adequate reafon why the fermons of many Prelates and Doctors, which have been *heard* with the greateft attention and rapture have been *read* with the moft flegmatick indifference and infenfibility. For it was impoffible to print in a perfect conjunction with the

flowing

My paufe is not of the firft kind, becaufe nothing can equal the riches of my fubject, but it is a compound of the two laft, and this is the elegant tranfition by which I pafs or rather glide on to the fecond head of this difcourfe, in which we propofed,

To confider this lamentable event, even the death of poor Yorick with refpect to thofe focieties or individuals to whom it is a moft affecting and irreparable lofs.

This head will be very fhort, when compared with the former.——You imagine perhaps, that I would humoroufly infinuate thereby, that the facetious Doctor's death,

N O T E.

flowing periods, the fine bufhy wigg, the venerable ·look foftened by an engaging fmile, the mellow, ftrong, and well-modulated voice, the flowing gown, the ftately perfon, the graceful attitude, and other fuch tranfitory ingredients of pulpit-eloquence. The portrait of the preacher prefixed to his fermons does not at all fupply this defect——fince it rarely exhibits any thing beyond a mere *Caput mortuum.*

is

is little lamented and deplored, and that he has left as many dry cheeks behind him as if he had been a King, or an Emperor. You miſtake me entirely, gentle hearers; the number of thoſe that deplore the annihilation of our late friend is very great. And if I am more brief than might be expected upon this doleful part of my doleful ſubject, I have my reaſons.—— That is all that I ſhall ſay at preſent upon the matter. ——

To return then to my ſubject —— the death of the late Dr. Y o r i c k is an unfortunate event

1ſt, For the *time-killers* in general ; a ſociety much more, I ſhould ſay, infinitely more numerous than that of their mortal enemies, the ſociety for promoting arts, commerce, and manufactures.

Weep, O weep for the death of Yo-r i c k, and the ſuffocation of Triſtram, ye male and female children of leiſure,
whom

whom want of employment, abundance of
high feeding, and paucity of ideas, cast into that lethargick dejection, or rather *inac-
tivity* of mind commonly called *vapours*;—
for the facetious biographer, whose decea'e
we lament, often rouzed you from this
wretched state. He used, one way or another, to put your spirits in a salutary flutter,
either by *winding* up your ——— imagi-
nations, by exercising your sagacity, or by
exciting your laughter. He would, had
his time been prolonged, have defended
you against *time* itself ; yes, against *time*,
that sluggish friend, which draws out your
insignificant existence to such a tedious
length, and which, though it dies daily under the barbarous blows you give it, yet
constantly resumes a new existence to re-
new your torment.——— You know, that
the *good* man had in a manner engaged himself to *write* as long as he *lived*, (y) and, in-

N O T E.

(y) " ——— being determined as long as I live
deed,

deed, if we confider the manner of treating his fubject that he has obferved hither-to ; any fubject, let it be what it may, would furnifh matter for innumerable vo-lumes to a pen like his. A man that could fill almoft three volumes with the life of his hero, before that hero was born (z) muft have been poffeffed of fuch a bat-tological fertility as nothing could exhauft. Here then, had YORICK lived, was a fine profpect for thofe *reading* time-killers, who cannot fupport their wretched exiftence, if it is not animated with a fucceffion of ob-jects that excite and fatisfy their curiofity, tickle their fancies, and enflame their paf-fions. In the flattering profpect of volume after volume for many fucceeding years, what a rich fund of entertainment was laid

N O T E S.

" or write, which in my cafe, means the fame
" thing ———" *Life and opinions of Triftram Shandy,*
vol. III. p. 16.

(z) If this refembles an Hibernian Bull, it muft be laid to the charge of him that occafioned it.

up for them ?—— All this profpect has di-
fappeared : YORICK writes, or at leaft,
prints no more, and therefore he is dead,
according to his own declaration.

I will not infift, 2*dly*, on the lofs which
the church has fuffered by the death of
YORICK, becaufe this is a point, which
I might not perhaps be able to render clear
and convincing to the generality of thofe
that fhall read my fermon, when it is printed ; tho' I think to you, my *worthy* hearers, (*a*) the matter muft be fufficiently evident.

It has been often obferved, that nothing
tends more to the credit of religion, than
purging it from thofe prejudices that difho-
nour its fimplicity. How free YORICK
was from all prejudices of every kind, is
well known. He had levelled them with
a Herculean hand. Nay, the common pre-
ju-

N O T E S.

(*a*) By his *worthy hearers*, Mr. FLAGELLAN here
underftood, without doubt, that part of his audience,
which comprehended the *Bucks* and *Jemmies*.

judices of education, which are the hard-
eft to conquer, and which tend to give
religion and morality a *defpotick* fway over
the hearts of men which were created *free*,
fell before his victorious arm. ——— I
don't like much to enlarge upon this to-
pick, ———there are ftill fome fqueamifh
ftomachs, which cannot digeft ftrong food ;
you underftand me ——— a word to the
wife is fufficient.

Need I mention, 3*dly*, the extraordinary
manner in which the death of our late
jovial friend muft affect the coffee-houfes
of London in particular, and Great Bri-
tain in general. There has of late been
obferved a remarkable ftagnation of prittle-
prattle and tittle-tattle in thefe promifcu-
ous abodes of heterogeneous mortals. The
coronation, indeed, revived a little the fpirit of loquacity, and fet many tongues a-
going. The news of a battle or defeat
produce now and then the fame effect. But
thefe are only incidental topicks of conver-

F 2   fa-

fation, which may ferve for a few days and
are foon exhaufted. The Miniftry, to the
forrow of thofe who are by nature Grumble-
tonians, are abfolutely above cenfure, and
the name of that virtuous and truly patriot
King, who now adorns the Britifh throne
cannot be pronounced without exciting the
warmeft fentiments of love and veneration,
and the fincereft effufions of applaufe. But
we generally are more prone to cenfure than
to praife. And even when we praife, we
dont love to praife long. So that King and
miniftry, after being praifed for a while
with much verbofity on account of the *novelty* as well as the *greatnefs* of the merit
which they difplay in their high fpheres,
will foon become the objects of *filent* veneration and efteem. Britons in this age are
like the Athenians of old, they are always
in fearch of fomething new, to arouze their
loquacity, and though, indeed, it was very
new, to fee fuch a king, and two fuch mi-
nifters (*b*), yet it will we hope in time be o'd.

N O T E S.

(*b*) This was written before the late change in

May they see their hoary heads crowned with such honours, as shall animate the virtuous ambition of the rising generation to follow their examples. ———— Lord ! what a digreffion !———— You have not, however, forgot what I was saying.————

The coffee-houses want matter.— Oppofition, which was always a rich fource of fmall and big talk, being ftruck dumb, what was left to exercife the lungs of our vociferous cits, but *the life and opinions of Triftram Shandy ?* The events, incidents, attitudes, points of view, tales, reflections, apoftrophe's, digreffions, characters, hints, ftrokes, pufhes, touches, portraits, double entendres, lights, and fhades of that admirable work, would have furnifhed them converfation for many years, had its mortal author found the means of efcaping death and oblivion.

I haften, my brethren, (for I perceive that I grow prolix, and you perhaps may have perceived it long ago) to the IIId and laft

the miniftry, and Mr. FLAGELLAN hopes, that there is not, nor ever will be, reafon to change it, or to wifh it *un-written. Vicarius Braius.*

head

head of this difcourfe, in which I propofed
to anfwer the objections that have been mouthed and handed about againft the memory
and good fame of the deceafed. You will
now perhaps imagine within yourfelves that
this is the moft difficult part of my fubject,
and that I have undertaken here a tafk, beyond any man's power to execute. But here
you miftake entirely the matter——— and
I enter into this branch of my fermon with
the utmoft confidence, with the moft trium-
phant affurance.

I. Objection. Dr. *Yorick in writing a ro-*
mance, wrote upon a fubject foreign to his voca-
tion, and thereby grofly mifapplied his time.

Anfwer. If this were a real crime, Lord
have mercy upon the greateft part of us !
for perhaps no crime was ever fo general in
our days, as that of writing, nay and living
too out of character. We might hide *Yorick*
from the force of this objection with the
numbers that are in the fame cafe, and fay
with *Juvenal,*

Defendit.numerus, junctæque ambone Phalanges.

It

It may be farther obferved, that perfons may be extremely unfit for the duties of a vocation, into which they are thrown by chance, intereft, or fuch-like caufes; and when they are unfit for the duties of their own vocation, is it not rather laudable than criminal to act in foreign characters? Is not this better than not to act at all?——This was precifely the cafe of YORICK. Neither *nature* nor *grace* had called him to be a Minifter of Chrift: yet he *fortuitoufly* or *cunningly* became a Parfon in fpite of both. In this new and ill-fuited character he looked like a *Bacchanal* in a *hermitage*, and faid firft to himfelf and afterwards to the world;

Naturam expellas furca licet ufque recurret. His cabinet became the nurfery of a romance, and his life——fomething more fubftantial. This is fomewhat obfcure,—— the fpirit of Triftram was again coming upon me —— avaunt thou fiend of *darknefs vifible.*

But after all, we reft our caufe here upon the ftrength of numbers, and only alledge that *Yorick* was not criminal in taking up

an

an *occupation* foreign to his profeſſion, ſince many are in the ſame caſe, who are not even accuſed. Who ever reproached the Reverend Mr. P - - - - p F - - - - - s, with ſpending the flower and ſtrength of his days in tranſlating and commenting the odes, epodes, ſatires and epiſtles of that agreeable and elegant rake *Horace*, though it is plain that his vocation pointed out to him ſtudies and occupations of a quite different nature? Who ever blamed the very learned and ghoſtly Chancellor of L-----n for ſpending thoſe precious moments upon the orations of Demoſthenes that his profeſſion demanded for the diſcourſes and precepts of his Great Maſter, *who ſpoke as never man ſpoke?* (c) We ſhall not ſpeak of the ingenious

N O T E S.

(c) This was the eminent Divine, who at the end of a laborious book, which contained an elegant mix-ture of *Civil Law* and *Philology*, added his lucubrations upon an old piece of moulded copper, and in theſe lucubrations attempted to prove to the great aſtoniſh-ment of *Hiſtory* and *common ſenſe* (who turned their aſ-toniſhment into laughter when they had heard his
argu-

nious author of the Roscıad, —— becaufe we diftinguifh between an *amufement* and an *occupation*; though we might of the moft critical and Greek learned bifhop who is about to give us another bad edition of Longinus. It would be endlefs to mention the number of Divines who have been fweating over the Polytheift *Homer*, the Atheift *Lucretius* and the Epicurean *Virgil*, while West and Littleton were writing upon the Refurrection of Chrift and the Converfion of the Glorious Apoftle of the Gentiles. (*b*)——Such then being the ftate of the cafe, why fhould Yorick be re-

G   proach-

N O T E S.

arguments) that the firft chriftians were not perfecut-ed for their *Religion*, but for their *noêturnal affemblies*, ——and that perfecution for religious opinions grew firft in a chriftian foil. *Afconius Benthicarius.*

(*b*) It is not to be imagined that Mr. Flacellan has here mentioned the late excellent Mr. West, and the truly learned and worthy Peer whofe name is here joined with his, as perfons, writing out of their pro-feffion. No,——they wrote in a character, which both their writings and their lives have difplayed in

ies

proached for doing, what so many have done with impunity? Why should he be blamed for sending to his garret or the snuff-shop the Bible, the Fathers, the commentators, &c. and placing upon his reading-desk *Petronius* and *Rabelais, Cervantes,* and *Slawkenbergius.* —— You may not perhaps be acquainted with this latter.——It was the Gentleman who wrote the Chapter of Nofes, a chapter so famous for its perspicuity, sense, and decency; a chapter however, at which certain old-fashioned and un-initiated readers, not knowing whether they were to laugh or weep, struck the diagonal or middle-way —— and yawned ———— but with a frown. (*c*)

IId.

N O T E S.

its true colours, in the respectable character of christians. And they have contributed more to the support of the best of all causes, (which owes its present decay, rather to levity and voluptuousness, than reason and argument) than the two thirds of that Reverend Bench that nod at the head of a declining Church. *Warburtonius.*

(*c*) This shews the singular effect of the *Chapter of Nofes,* because according to the conformation of the muscles

IId. *Objection. Both the writings and dif-*
courfe of Dr. Yorick were larded with obfceni-
ties, and this is quite inconfiftent with the cha-
racter of a clergy-man.

Anfwer. There are two ways of eluding
the force of this objection. —— The *one* by
alledging, that *Yorick* was not *really* and
effentially a clergyman ; and then the objection is prevented ;——the *other*, by proving,
that he was not *obfcene* either in writings or
difcourfe, and then the objection is directly
deftroyed. —— If I cannot fufficiently make
out this fecond point, I fhall but trefs it with
a *third* in order to prove that obfcenity in
writing or difcourfe is not always a proof
that a man is either difhoneft or immoral.

The *firft* of thefe points does not demand
a long difcuffion. Its decifion depends
upon the definition of a *clergyman.* If by a
clergyman, you mean, a *two-legged animal,*
G 2 *without*

N O T E.

mufcles of the face, a yawn is moft naturally followed with a certain unmeaning ferenity of countenance,
which even approaches to a fmile. *Hillius Anatomico-*
Herbario-Ethico-dramatico-philologico-Theologico-Chymicus.

without feathers, of an erect posture, not less than four, nor more than seven foot high, with a great quantity of fictitious hair about his head that looks like the erected quills of an angry porcupine, together with a long black robe, and a white piece of cambrick under his chin, then it muft be acknowledged that according to this definition, the deceafed Doc·tor was *really* a clergy-man and therefore the objection under confideration is not yet prevented. But if befides the circumftances of being *two-legged, without feathers,* and the others now-mentioned, you comprehend in your definition, *piety of fentiment, dignity of behaviour, fanctity of manners, zeal for the advancement of religion and virtue,* and a *pre-vailing habit of decency and propriety* that does not even defert the hours of relaxation and pleafure, then the objection is prevent-ed; for according to this definition our de-ceafed Friend was not a clergyman. He, indeed, though in the fore moft rank, is not the only one whofe *indelible* character would be utterly effaced by this definition. It is a terrible definition, my brethren, would

prove

prove a fort of a *draw-canfir* among the fa-
cred legions of the Church, and deftroy the
clerical exiftence of thoufands.

But left you fhould cavil at the *nice* and
fubtile diftinction which I have here made
between a clergyman in one fenfe, and a
clergyman in another, I will not reft here
the defence of Poor *Yorick*, but *directly* deftroy the force of the objection by proving
that the deceafed was not obfcene neither
in his writings nor difcourfe. —— And here
I obferve,

In the *firft place*, that he was not obfcene
in his words. There is not a fingle word in
the life of Triftram Shandy, (if you will
except fome bye-words of Sergeant *Trim*,
and fome technical terms of Dr. *Slop*) that is
not to be found, without any note of infamy, in the dictionary of the learned, grave,
venerable and folemn Mr. *Samuel Johnfon.*
Nay, fo far did our departed friend carry his
delicacy on that head, that knowing that the
chafteft words might fometimes be the innocent occafion of exciting the fouleft ide-

as,

as, he expreffed himfelf frequently by a dafh ——————— without even ufing the initial letters, left fome wag more fagacious than his fellows fhould peep into his meaning.

If you alledge, that dafhes ————— are often very expreffive and clear when taken in their connexions, and that there are feveral phrafes in the book in queftion, that, pure as the words which compofe them may be, are yet, when taken together, expreffive of lafcivious operations and impure motions, I anfwer ; that this is unavoidable, unlefs we abandon the words that are the moft in ufe, and that are employed even by prudes themfelves. The terms *marriage, marriage-bed, wedding-night, pregnancy,* and many others convey precifely the fame ideas, which poor YORICK is blamed for having excited in feveral parts of his book. Do but analyfe thefe expreffions and the fentences in which they are employed every day, and you will find yourfelves juft where YORICK was leading your palpitating fancies, when he talked

talked of *winding up the old clock*, of the *stranger's cod-piece*, or of his *mother's not caring to let a man come so near her* * * * *. Are not the words *adultery, fornication*, and the like pronounced every day by the purest mouths, and where is the vestal that does not talk without a blush of the village of *Maiden-head*, of *Petticoat-lane*, where we are at present assembled, tho' we need not insinuate the collateral and accessory ideas which start up at the pronunciation of these innocent terms? The historian *Mezerai* tells us of a priest, who had been surprized in bed with his neighbour's wife, and who was punished by the lopping off the *parts* which had committed *the crime*. This is speaking plainly enough. A Dash would not have said more, and yet *Mezerai* passes for a chaste and wise writer.

You will alledge, perhaps, that YORICK spoke of, and hinted at these impure objects, without necessity, thro' choice, from a spirit of wantonness, and without any other design than to tickle the fancy at the expence of virtue. This side of the objection perplexes me a good deal;

deal; the anfwer to it is fomewhat difficult,
I therefore pafs on to my third and laft ob-
fervation, which is,

That obfcenity in writing or difcourfe is not
always a proof that a man is either difhoneft
or immoral ; But as I perceive (*Here Mr. Flagellan fhook the fand-glafs*) that your time is
elapfed, and that this point would require a
very long difcuffion, before we could draw any
thing from it to the advantage of the deceafed, we fhall not enter upon it at prefent, nor
perhaps in any future time, but conclude as we
propofed, with an *improper* application of what
has been faid.

. Let us learn from the annihilation of Yo-
RICK, that licentious wit is a bubble, and that
ill-got fame is a capricious ftrumpet, whofe
uncertain and tranfitory fmiles portend future
infamy and contempt, while decency and virtue are the fureft paths to true honour, will,
fooner or later captivate the reluctant applaufe
of the moft worthlefs, and be perfectly happy,
without it, in the efteem of the wife and good.

F I N I S.